ENGAGING THE FAMILY: REUNION PLANNING MADE SIMPLE

A STEP-BY-STEP PROCESS FOR PLANNING YOUR FAMILY REUNION

BETTIE J. MILLEDGE

ENGAGING THE FAMILY: REUNION PLANNING MADE SIMPLE

Copyright @ 2021 by Bettie J. Milledge

DESTA (Development, Educational Support, Training and Assessment)

All rights reserved. No part of this publication may be reproduced, distributed or transmitted in any form or by any means, including photocopying, recording, or other electronic or mechanical methods, without the prior written permission of the publisher, except in the case of brief quotations embodied in critical reviews and certain other noncommercial uses permitted by copyright law.

Although the author and publisher have made every effort to ensure that the information in this book was correct at press time, the author and publisher do not assume and hereby disclaim any liability to any part for any loss, damage, or disruption caused by errors or omissions, whether such errors or omissions result from negligence, accident, or any other cause. Any perceived slight of any individual or organization is purely unintentional.

Adherence to all applicable laws and regulations, including international, federal, state, and local governing professional licensing, business practices, advertising, and all other aspects of doing business in the US, Canada or any other jurisdiction is the sole responsibility of the reader and consumer.

Neither the author nor the publisher can be held responsible for the use of the information provided within this book. Please always consult a trained professional before making any decision regarding treatment of yourself or others.

ISBN: 978-1-7360180-3-3 Paperback

ISBN: 978-1-7360180-2-6 ebook

GET YOUR GIFT!

One-Page Task Checklist

This one-page task checklist provides new planners with essential areas to target when planning a family reunion. The checklist monitors five key areas.

1. Task Achievement
2. Targeted Timelines
3. Self-Monitoring
4. Tracking of New Tasks
5. Tracking Required Follow-up

To claim your gift, go to www.bettiespeaks.com and follow the instructions.

CONTENTS

Dedication   vii
Introduction   xi

1. Engaging Family And Setting The Tone   1
2. Planning Your Reunion   5
3. Reunion Structure   15
4. Reunion Planning Team   20
5. Reunion Registration   30
6. Reunion Events   35
7. Reunion Budget   45
8. Reunion Monitoring   50
9. Board of Directors   53
10. Assessing the Reunion   67

Index of Forms   69
Acknowledgments   91
About the Author   93
Can You Help?   95

Dedication

I WANT TO DEDICATE THIS BOOK TO MY SON, ALVIN WOODARD, III. His spirit was an inspiration to me in every area of this book. Although his life on this Earth was short, it had purpose. He loved God, his family, and his friends.

Alvin displayed his love for his family and friends through his giving. I laugh and cry when I think about his loving ways. He was truly a giver. I remember the times when he literally gave the shirt off his back, gave away his lunch money and lunches, and gave his little savings to help family members and friends. Those memories of love will always be with me.

Father God, I thank you for allowing me to be Alvin's mother.

COMMENTS ABOUT OUR FAMILY REUNIONS

1992-Romulus (Detroit), Michigan: The reunion was fantastic! I had the opportunity to meet a guest who was 103 years of age. She was one of ten distinguished head-table guests. The reunion displayed love for family and friends. I had a great time and enjoyed the reunion.
Mary Jackson – Detroit, Michigan

2000-Davenport, Iowa: We had a wonderful time at the reunion in Davenport, Iowa. Met new family members attending reunion for the first time. Reunions are a great time to hang out with family and friends. We love attending our family reunions and have not missed any of them.
The Farries Family – Hiram, Georgia

2010-Atlanta, Georgia: Best part of the Atlanta reunion was just simply being there! The auction and activities were great. Reunion hosted by the Farries Family – wonderful time was had by all. There was a large turnout of family and friends. Some of our family attending the reunion are no longer with us, but not forgotten. Accommodations were simply marvelous. Atlanta – a great city to host the reunion.
Steve, Jackie, and Tristian Joiner – Memphis, Tennessee

<u>2014-St. Louis, Missouri</u>: I have attended several of the Turner-Ford Family Reunions. It is hard to describe the Food! Entertainment! Love! Attending these reunions gave me a sense of what is truly the most important thing in life – "the love of family."
Ebonie M. Smith – Chicago, Illinois

<u>2016-New Orleans, Louisiana</u>: Great reunion! Enjoyed the activities, especially the auction. The location was ideal. I was able to visit my family.
Ronny Young – Arlington, Texas

<u>2016-New Orleans, Louisiana</u>: This reunion, as well as others, brought joy to my heart. The reunions are always lots of fun and great activities. I love to get with my family and just spend good old family time together. New Orleans is a great place to have a family reunion.
Marvin Joiner – Memphis, Tennessee

<u>2018-Tinley Park, Illinois</u>: The Voices, an entertainment group, was the highlight of the reunion. The family had a great time. The food was fantastic. Overall, the family was the most important part of the reunion.
The Bell Family – Chicago, Illinois

INTRODUCTION

In 1989, I had dinner with several family members in Romulus, Michigan. As we ate, we had a passionate and interactive discussion regarding family reunions. My Aunt Renee from Racine, Wisconsin asked, "Why don't we have family reunions?"

Knowing her sense of humor, I responded by saying, "We don't have family reunions because we can't stand being around each other for more than two or three days." Of course, I was joking, and everyone laughed, including my Aunt Renee.

Although she laughed loudly, her comments were direct and to the point. She replied in a demanding voice, "You are probably right, but we need to have family reunions, and you, Bettie, will be the chairperson for our reunions."

Introduction

The laughter continued, and they all agreed with the "demand." That enjoyable dinner in 1989 was the beginning of the Turner-Ford Family Reunion planning process.

As a team, we planned our first family reunion. Our reunion plans came to fruition during the third weekend of July 1990 when 94 family members and friends gathered in Memphis, Tennessee. The participants represented 11 cities and 6 states. It thrilled us to see family members so excited. They showed their spirit of love with hugs, kisses, laughter, and shared memories.

At the end of the reunion, the team came together to review the evaluation sheets and verbal feedback we received from the reunion participants. In these evaluations, the family suggested we write guidelines for future reunions. In response, we formed a committee to write reunion guidelines in 1993. The next year, the family approved the guidelines. We have seen a steady increase in reunion participation since implementing these guidelines.

Since the first reunion in 1990, we have had a 34% increase in participation, with 276 attending in 2018. The 276 participants represented 51 cities and 19 states. This increase of family participation did not happen by chance, but through deliberate engagement with family members focused on communicating, planning, organizing, and executing plans to ensure a successful reunion.

The experience of witnessing families connecting and reconnecting during each of our family reunions has been amazing. Many of the new connections still continue and

Introduction

have extended beyond the reunions. For our family, reunion planning has been very rewarding. The level of enthusiasm by the planners and the family's anticipation of the fun activities is everlasting. Over the years, our family members and friends have been the recipients of intentional love and the commitment to connect and reconnect during each reunion.

After reading this book, you can have the same success in planning your family reunions. Although it provides information and tools for first-time planners, it can also serve as a resource for experienced planners. This book will guide planners from a desire and commitment to host a reunion to executing plans and celebrating a new family tradition, while keeping you focused and on task.

It is important to understand that you should plan a reunion in a specific sequence. Planners should go through the chapters in order, following the step-by-step process. Throughout the book, you will find the information you need to start planning, including processes for selecting a venue, a sample registration package, a sample budget with a detailed checklist for monitoring tasks and achievements, and much, much more.

There are so many reasons for having a family reunion. It is truly a wonderful opportunity to show appreciation, catch up on old times, share exciting things happening with family and friends, and to celebrate each other.

The following quotes provide our family with inspiration and energy as we plan and gather together. I hope they will

Introduction

also serve as an inspiration to you as you begin your family reunion tradition.

"Love your family, share the blessings God blessed you with."
DOROTHY MAE WHITE-TURNER, AGE 90

"You don't choose your family – they are God's gift to you, as you are to them."
DESMOND TUTU, AFRICAN LEADER OF THE ANTIAPARTHEID STRUGGLE

CHAPTER 1
ENGAGING FAMILY AND SETTING THE TONE

Chapter Preview

- Introduction to the Chapter
- Methods of Getting Family Input
- Reunion's Foundation for Vision and Goals
- Chapter Summary: Key Areas Addressed

The primary strategies for planning a family reunion are engaging your family and setting the tone for participation. In this chapter, we will discuss the importance of these strategies.

When preparing for a family reunion, it can be gratifying to engage with your family, and it can also help things run smoother. Over the past 40+ years, I have engaged family members in planning activities for students, organizing outings for company employees, designing interactive activities for physically challenged individuals, and planning family reunions. I learned strategies for engaging families early in my career as a teacher, through celebrating student achievements in my classroom. The benefits included:

1. Increased levels of parental participation.
2. Increased student engagement.
3. Increased completion of assignments.
4. Increased student happiness in anticipating celebrations.

The other strategy we utilize in planning our reunions is setting the tone. Setting the tone is a continual process throughout the preparation, planning, and execution of plans for a reunion. It is an essential strategy that contributes to establishing relationships that begin with input from family members.

There are a variety of methods for getting family input. For example, you can get input through conversations with family members or through feedback from reunion attendees. We carefully assess input from family members and friends as we plan our reunions. We decided several years ago to address input from family and friends, even in the form of questions, promptly. Over the years, the team has faced questions such as those listed below.

1. Will there be an increase in the reunion fees?
2. What can we do to help keep the reunion fees low?
3. Why are our reunions every two years?
4. Why can't we have our next reunion on a cruise ship?
5. Who manages the reunion money?

After realizing the importance of engaging the family and setting the tone, we moved forward with formalizing our reunion planning process. We formed an ad hoc team to establish the purpose of the reunion and developed a logistical plan to research and contact family members to gauge their interest in the reunion. The team addressed questions presented by family members and friends.

We continued to move ahead with our purpose in mind. This purpose later became the foundation for our vision and goals, outlined below.

Vision

To host family reunions that will connect and reconnect family members living throughout the world.

Goals

1. To implement strategies that intentionally engage our biological and extended family members.

2. To use proven procedures and tools in planning the family reunions.
3. To plan and host affordable reunions and provide start-up money for future reunions.

Chapter 1 Summary: Key Areas addressed

- The two primary strategies for planning a family reunion are engaging family and setting the tone for participation.
- When preparing for a family reunion, it's gratifying to engage with the family. Also, by engaging with the family, it is easier to reach your desired outcomes.
- Setting the tone is a continual process throughout the preparation, planning, and execution of plans for a reunion.
- Input from family and friends, even in the form of questions, should be addressed in a reasonable amount of time.
- The purpose of the reunion, which is to connect and reconnect family members, became the foundation for the vision and goals.

CHAPTER 2

PLANNING YOUR REUNION

Chapter Preview

- Introduction to the Chapter
- Recommended Steps for Planning Your First Reunion
- Recommended Meeting Strategies
- Experienced Reunion Planners
- Chapter Summary: Key Areas Addressed
- Sample Family Reunion Survey Form (See Index of Forms)

Although planning a family reunion may seem daunting, it is simple when you have the required resources. The Six Steps for First-Time Reunion Planners, listed below, will help new planners get started. Do not be intimidated! If you have the desire to plan your first reunion and commit to each step of the process, you are on the path to having a successful event.

Step 1: Share Desire and Commitment

The first step to planning your family reunion is your desire and commitment. You want to keep an optimistic outlook as you engage your family members. Keep in mind your desire is to plan a family reunion, and you will need family members to help you along the way. Be sure to choose your family helpers wisely and share with them your goals and optimism. You want to stay away from joy killers. These are individuals who will have nothing positive to say about what you want to achieve. If you want to have a family reunion, it is likely that other members of your family will feel the same way. Continue sharing your desire and commitment, and you will connect with those family members ready to help you with the reunion.

Step 2: Conduct Survey

Engaging family members in a quick survey can be an excellent indicator of those interested in planning a reunion. Take into account, every family member you contact will not share your enthusiasm for a family reunion. Do not lose hope and stop if you receive a negative response. Keep the optimism going until you get 10 to 12 positive responses. In the Index of Forms, you will locate the sample Family Survey

Form. This sample form will help you get started. Once you complete the surveys, the positive family members should be your group for the next step.

Step 3: Host a Group Meeting

The greater the number of family members taking part in the group meeting, the more likelihood there will be a significant number who will commit to help plan the family's first reunion. Be aware, a group meeting can get intense when individuals are trying to share their own points of view. Therefore, the host should consider using certain strategies (I recommend several below) to achieve the intended purpose of the meeting.

Meeting Strategies

- Be sure to have an agenda for each meeting.
- Engage family members in the process by thanking them for attending the meeting.
- Share the purpose of the meeting. Share your desire to have a reunion.
- Discuss feedback from the surveys.
- Ask open-ended questions about having a family reunion. (Example: What are your thoughts about having a family reunion?)
- Allow individuals to share their thoughts without interruption.

- Share enjoyable stories about elderly and young family members.
- Get the group excited about a reunion by repeating your desire to have one.
- Express a willingness to host the first reunion with help from the group.
- Other strategies as needed.

Step 4: Use Informal Structure

The informal structure is most often used for family reunion planning. This structure has a more flexible style of leadership. It allows the planning team to make all decisions for the family reunion, which include selecting the venue and establishing the reunion budget. Based on a survey of nine families using the informal structure, the rational for choosing this structure included the comments listed below.

1. Flexibility of leadership and planning team
2. Small family group, less than 125 participants
3. Location for reunion usually does not change
4. Leadership and planning team generally do not change

The planning team operating under the informal structure is responsible for securing the start-up funds for the reunion. The start-up funds usually include deposits for venues and vendors. Under this structure, I recommend the two options.

Option 1: The planning team loans money to the reunion for start-up costs, and requests repayment at the conclusion of the event.

Option 2: The planning team seeks donations from family members to cover the start-up costs.

Step 5: Establish Your Planning Team

The Planning Team is key to planning a successful reunion and must work as a unit. Often, the team leader will group team members to determine similarities in work styles. The grouping of team members also helps them become familiar with each other's work, personality, and skill sets. When you know each person's skills, you can put together more efficient groups.

The team should become familiar with the Eight Tips for a Planning Team listed below. The Eight Tips provide invaluable information regarding the role of the team in addressing key areas for a reunion.

Tip #1: Select dates(s) for the reunion.

Family input in selecting dates for the reunion is important; however, if this is your first reunion, the planning team typically selects reunion dates. At the conclusion of the first reunion, the family usually selects the dates for the second reunion. Holidays are a great time to have family reunions. The most popular holiday for a reunion is July 4th.

Tip #2: Select a location for the reunion.

The planning team has the responsibility of selecting a location for the reunion, especially if it is the first reunion. The planning team will decide the activities for the reunion, which will contribute to the decision regarding location. They should consider the questions listed below, and others when asking, "How do you select a location for a family reunion?"

Questions

- In what city and state will we host the reunion?
- Can the location accommodate the needs of the group?
- Are family members from other cities and states planning to attend the reunion?
- What is the estimated number of reunion participants?
- How many days are planned for the reunion?
- What types of activities are planned for the reunion?

- Will reunion participants need overnight accommodations?
- Is the location available on the date(s) planned for the reunion?

Tip #3: Survey the Venue

The planning team should survey venues prior to selecting one. Surveys can start with a phone conversation but should result in an on-site visit prior to a final decision. The venue must be able to accommodate the activities planned for the reunion. The eight questions listed above will help the team in surveying venues. Use the sample venue form provided in the Index of Forms and conduct a phone survey. When the team completes the surveys, compile the data, and select your top three venues.

Tip #4: Meet with the Venue Representatives

Members of the planning team should meet with representatives from the top three venue choices. The team must be prepared for each meeting, to include a list of questions, survey results, and be ready to interact with venue representatives. The interaction should include a tour while asking specific questions.

Tip #5: Meet with the Planning Team

Following the meeting with the venue representatives of all three venues, the entire planning team should meet to discuss each venue and make a decision.

Tip #6: Venue Selection

When the planning team is prepared to select a venue, the team leader should contact the venue representative via phone and express a desire to enter into a contract with the venue.

Tip #7: Letter of Intent

The team leader should make sure everything agreed upon during the meeting with the venue representative is stated in the Letter of Intent. The purpose of this document is to officially notify the venue of the family's wishes before finalizing the reservation.

Tip #8: Negotiating the Contract

The team will receive two contracts, a proposed contract, and a final contract. The team leader should review each contract, using a checklist, to make sure the items agreed upon (during the meetings and further discussions) are in the document. The team leader will notify the venue representative of any concerns, and schedule a follow-up meeting, if there are changes needed. The team leader will sign the final contract.

Step 6: Establish Reunion Fee and Budget

The team should plan for reunion fees in advance. They should establish age group ranges and the fees for each group. Examples of age groups are: 17 years and older, 14-15 years, 11-13 years, 8-10 years, 4-7 years, and 3 years and under. The planning team must project a realistic number of participants for each age group based on communication with family members. The estimated number of participants for each age group, multiplied by the fee for each age group provides an overall forecast of income for the proposed budget. Budget revisions usually occur at least two or three times when planning a reunion.

Chapter 2 Summary: Key Areas Addressed

- The Six Steps for First-Time Reunion Planners, listed below, will assist planners in getting started.

Step 1. Sharing your desire and commitment
Step 2. Conducting a survey
Step 3. Hosting a group meeting
Step 4. Using informal structure
Step 5. Establishing a planning team

Step 6. Establishing your reunion fees by age group and reunion budget

- The Eight Tips for a Planning Team, listed below, provide invaluable information regarding the role of the team in planning a reunion.

Tip #1: Select dates for the reunion
Tip #2: Select location for the reunion
Tip #3: Survey the venue for the reunion
Tip #4: Meet with venue representative
Tip #5: Meet with the planning team
Tip #6: Select venue for the reunion
Tip #7: Develop a Letter of Intent
Tip #8: Negotiate the contract

- The sample form, Family Reunion Survey, is an example used for my Family reunions. The form is located in the Index of Forms.

CHAPTER 3
REUNION STRUCTURE

Chapter Preview

- Introduction to the Chapter
- Informal Structure Description
- Formal Structure Description
- Request to Host Reunion Procedures
- Request Approval Process
- Chapter Summary: Key Areas Addressed
- Sample Request to Host Reunion Form (See Index of Forms)

The structure of a reunion is the organizational system or style of leadership used to plan and execute plans for a reunion. The goal is to have a successful reunion. Some reunion planners may like total control in decision-making, while others may like support. In the end, the family needs to decide on the reunion structure.

The two structures, detailed below, are similar with the primary difference being the support from a board of directors with clearly defined roles and responsibilities, as opposed to a planning team having total control in decision-making in all areas.

Informal Structure:

Informal structure is most often used by families planning family reunions. It has a more flexible style of leadership. Here are some reasons to use an informal structure:

- Only local family members and friends take part in the reunion.
- The reunion is a one-day event.
- Only a small group is taking part.
- The planning team makes all the decisions.
- There is greater flexibility in leadership and the planning team.
- The location does not change for the reunion.

Formal Structure:

The formal structure provides two levels of decision-making. One level is the board of directors, and the second level is the local planning team. Although there are two levels of decision-making, the board and local planning team are collaborative decision-makers in planning and hosting reunions.

The formal structure is a clearly defined system explaining roles, responsibilities, and rules. We have procedures regarding how information flows from the board to planning team, and then to family and friends in all areas of the reunion-planning process.

Changing from an informal structure to a formal structure requires preparation. We made the switch over a two-year period. Our formal structure includes an eleven-member board of directors that helps the local team with each family reunion. This structure shows how the engagement of family members helps to achieve the vision and goals established for our family reunions. Reunion data was a key factor in deciding to change to a formal system.

Request to Host Family Reunion:

Within the formal structure, a board of directors decides when to host a reunion. In order to present your request to the board, the team leader must notify a board member prior to the board meeting.

Following the verbal notification, the team leader completes the Request to Host Family Reunion Form. They submit the request to a board member prior to the board meeting. (See request form in the Index of Forms). All requests are reviewed by the board prior to the banquet.

Approval Process:

During the banquet, at a designated time, the general chairperson presents the request(s) to host the next reunion.

The family and friends vote to determine the team to host the next reunion when more than one request is made. Whichever team obtains the most votes will be approved to host the next reunion. If no voting is required, the requesting team (to host the reunion) is introduced to the family. They communicate the location and dates for the next reunion to family and friends.

Engaging family members and friends in determining reunion locations has the potential to increase participation. Family members, in most cases, have area they are fond of and enjoy returning to those locations. This also encourages other family members to attend along with their friends.

At this point, you have completed the third chapter and are probably starting to think about the structure for your next reunion. As you dive into Chapter 4, you will better understand how the structures impact a reunion.

Chapter 3 Summary: Key Areas Addressed

- The two structures discussed in this chapter are informal and formal.
- The informal structure is most often used by families in planning family reunions, and has a more flexible style of leadership.

- The formal structure has two levels of decision-making: a board of directors and a reunion planning team.
- Changing your reunion structure from informal to formal requires preparation. In order to determine which structure is best for your family, you should use your reunion data.
- The sample form "Request to Host Family Reunion" is an example used for our family reunion. This form is located in the Index of Forms.

CHAPTER 4

REUNION PLANNING TEAM

Chapter Preview

- Introduction to the Chapter
- 8 Tips for Your Planning Team
- Definition of a Skill Set
- Item Checklist for Venue Contract
- Chapter Summary: Key Areas Addressed
- Sample Venue Survey Form (See Index of Forms)

The reunion planning team plays a significant role in planning a family reunion. Team members must work together to successfully plan and host the event. As you seek team members, keep this John Maxwell quote in mind:

"Teamwork makes the dream work, but a vision becomes a nightmare when the leader has a big dream and a bad team."

When team members work together, they develop relationships and a variety of skill sets. The team leader and team members bring a variety of skills to the planning process. Skill sets are a combination of knowledge, personal qualities, and abilities that a person develops throughout their life and work. They include skills such as communicating, planning, managing, organizing, researching, consulting, and accounting. Often, the team leader will pair team members based on their skill sets. This process allows the team leader to assign planning tasks where skill sets complement each other, increasing efficiency. Efficiency and collaboration are critical in planning a family reunion.

A successful reunion results from the leadership and team members working together. The term successful can mean different things to different people; however, from this perspective, the term successful means achieving the goals and objectives established by the planning team.

Eight Tips for the Planning Team

Tip #1: Select date(s) for the reunion

Family input in selecting dates for a reunion is important. The family should also establish alternative date(s) for the reunion in the event the requested date(s) are not available. It is important to select reunions dates early. When dates are established early, it allows family and friends adequate time to plan accordingly. Securing early date(s) can also increase participation at a family reunion. Confirming date(s) for a family reunion should be a top priority.

Tip #2: Select location for the reunion

Depending on the reunion's structure, the location may require a vote by family members. You should give considerable thought to the location of your reunion. You want a location that brings a level of excitement to family members. For example, the location for our 2020 family reunion was ideal, although the reunion was cancelled because of COVID-19. We estimated that 75% of family members targeted to attend the reunion were from cities in proximity to the selected location. This decision supported engaging the family.

Tip #3: Survey potential venues

Planners should give a lot of thought to the reunion venue and consider the needs of family and friends. There are areas to be addressed throughout the venue survey process. The recommended questions below will start the process.

- Are the dates available?
- What is the level of security for the hotel?
- How soon can we tour the facility?
- Are sleeping rooms available for inspection?
- Is the staff customer friendly?
- What is the hotel's policy regarding visitors?
- What is the hotel's rating?
- Is a deposit required to secure the facility?
- Are meal prices negotiable for a banquet?
- Are daily meals (breakfast, lunch, dinner) served in the hotel?

You want to use your time wisely when searching for a venue. A brainstorming session regarding venues is usually an excellent place to start. The team can put together a list of venues, locations, and features to consider. They should also contact family members and friends regarding venues they have used for other events.

The sample venue survey form, located in the Index of Forms, should assist you in getting started with these tasks.

Following the completion of the surveys, the planning team should prioritize venues and begin the selection process, which starts with meeting a venue representative.

Tip #4: Meet with the venue representative

Preparation for a meeting with each selected venue should include a meeting agenda, a written list of questions, and the survey results. I recommend the team leader and at least two team members attend the meeting. You should assign designated questions to each team member and to the team leader. The team leader is the facilitator of the meeting and should follow an established agenda to ensure the group addresses all of your concerns. The overall goal is to prepare for the selection of the venue.

Tip #5: Meet with the planning team

Following the meeting with the venue representatives, the entire planning team should meet and discuss the outcomes of the meetings. The meeting notes with each representative are essential in selecting a venue and should confirm agreements and areas of follow up.

Tip #6: Select the venue

If the planning team is functioning under the formal structure, the general chairperson, treasurer, and team leader will make the final decision regarding the venue. If the planning team is functioning under the informal structure, the planning team will decide on the venue. Regardless of your reunion's structure, once you decide on a venue, the team leader should notify the venue representative immediately, via phone, of the intent to reserve the venue.

The planning team should maintain a communication log for all phone conferences. The log should reflect dates, persons contacted, approximate time(s), summaries of the discussion, and any agreements made. It is also imperative that a copy of all documents be maintained for easy access. This is especially helpful in the event of a change in venue representative assigned to the reunion planning team. The communication log will ensure a much smoother transition to a newly assigned venue representative.

Tip #7: Develop a Letter of Intent

The Letter of Intent can be critical in formalizing a contract. While it is a tool rarely used by planners for family reunions, the content of the document (Letter of Intent) should be based on the agreements captured from the meeting with the planning team and venue representative.

The team leader should follow up with the venue representative, establish a meeting date to discuss the Letter of Intent, and request an approximate date to receive the proposed contract. The team leader may choose not to meet with the representative prior to receiving the proposed contract.

Tip #8: Negotiate the Contract

A contract has legal terminology. It is important that your team understands the contract and that there is transparency (no hidden regulations) between the venue and the planning team.

Proposed Contract

The team should review the proposed contract, which is the initial contract based on information from the Letter of Intent and other documents (i.e., notes from meeting, etc.). The team leader should be the primary individual communicating with the venue representative.

Under the formal structure, the team leader should communicate with the general chairperson regarding the proposed contract. After the team leader reviews the proposed contract, and concerns are addressed, if any, the next step should be to follow-up with the planning team to review the proposed contract.

Be sure to review all areas of the proposed contract. Use a checklist, such as the one listed below. The proposed contract should reflect those items, if you made an agreement.

Item Checklist

- Reunion date(s)
- Hotel room rates and blocked date(s)
- Number of hotel rooms blocked for each date requested
- Reunion activities to be posted on the Hotel Event Board
- Number of proposed attendees (flexibility to

decrease or increase attendees within 15 days of the event)
- Special meal rates (quoted rates stated in document)
- Tax and gratuity for food and other items
- Layout for the banquet room (approved floor plan)
- Request for a head table (clarify if standard or elevated)
- Space for photographer with a back-drop, plus one six-foot table and two chairs
- Space for registration with two six-foot tables and four chairs
- One six-foot table and two chairs for the DJ
- Four six-foot tables for auction gifts
- Layout for the banquet (buffet or formal dinner – whichever scheduled)
- Dance floor (specify size)
- Banquet contact person
- Timeframe for meal (buffet or formal dinner)
- Meal replenishing frequency (if buffet)
- One six-foot table for memorial commemoration

If there are any requested changes to the contract, the team leader should communicate the requests to the venue representative within two to three days, in writing.

Signed Contract

The signed contract is the official document. It should represent the final agreements, including any requested changes noted in the proposed contract. Regardless of your reunion's structure, informal or formal, the signed contract represents a legal commitment. It is in the team's best interest to make sure the final document is acceptable and fully understood prior to signing. When the contract is signed, it becomes a legally binding agreement, and is usually enforceable in a court of law. Please know what you are signing.

Team members are invaluable and must be appreciated for their dedication, commitment, and work. The team will affect every area of the reunion.

Chapter 4 Summary: Key Areas Addressed

- The planning team plays a significant role in planning a family reunion.
- Often, a team leader will pair team members based on their skill sets.
- Skill sets are a combination of knowledge, personal qualities, and abilities that a person develops throughout their life and work.
- The Eight Tips for a Planning Team, listed below, provide essential information for the reunion planning team.

Tip # 1. Select the date(s) for the reunion.

Tip # 2. Select a location for the reunion.

Tip # 3. Survey the venue: Use the sample questions when interviewing the representative.

Tip # 4. Meet with a venue representative. Be prepared for the meeting.

Tip # 5. Meet with the planning team using an established agenda.

Tip # 6. Select a venue based on predetermined criteria.

Tip # 7. Develop a Letter of Intent based on agreements.

Tip # 8. Negotiate a contract based on agreements, including areas in the Letter of Intent.

- The sample form "Venue Survey" is an example used for my family reunion. This sample form is located in the Index of Forms.

CHAPTER 5
REUNION REGISTRATION

Chapter Preview

- Introduction to the Chapter
- Tracking Areas for Future Planning
- Impact of Inadequate Information
- Sample of Areas Required for Registration
- Chapter Summary: Key Areas Addressed
- Sample Reunion Letter (See Index of Forms)
- Sample Reunion Registration Form (See Index of Forms)
- Sample Reunion T-Shirt Form (See Index of Forms)
- Sample Request for Auction Gift Form (See Index of Forms)

Registration for a family reunion should be an organized process. It starts with confirmation of key information families and friends need to register for the reunion. Registration can feel hectic, but with the right tools and the implementation of proven strategies, it is not as bad as it seems.

At this point, we have developed the foundation for reunion registration. I introduced you to the processes in previous chapters addressing the reunion dates, location, venue, contract, and group fees. Now that you know the required information, the team can develop the registration package with the essential details.

As you develop the registration package, keep in mind that you should also develop a tracking system for registration. This can be as simple as creating a large binder with tabs or as complex as digitizing your data; whichever system you select, be sure to make it easily accessible. As you address the tracking system, determine areas that will be helpful in planning future reunions.

Sample tracking areas for future planning

1. Payment of reunion fees by age groups
2. Hometowns and states of reunion participants
3. Number of additional hotel rooms requested within cut-off reunion date
4. Number of t-shirts ordered by size

5. Number of gifts donated (auction and raffle)
6. Comments and recommendations regarding the reunion
7. Volunteers for reunion activities

Tracking registration is a vital part of planning a reunion, which keeps the planning team on target. When using the informal structure, the planning team selects the registration tracking system. Under the formal structure, the treasurer and general chairperson selects the tracking system. The lack of a tracking system for registration has implications for a financial disaster.

Registration for family reunions involves multiple tasks, usually requiring collaboration of several team members. Registration information must be accurate. Misinformation causes multiple problems such as family confusion, increased reunion expenses, tension amongst team members, delays in targeted dates or task completion, and much, much more.

You should also consider mailing dates for the registration packages when planning target dates. Mailing out registration packages should be a top priority. Delayed information may affect attendance at the reunion, unnecessary phone calls, emails, and family tension.

The sample registration package consists of four documents. They are Reunion Letter, Registration Form, T-shirt Form, and Request for Auction Gift Form. These sample documents, located in the Index of Forms, will guide the planning team in developing forms for registration. The reunion plan generally determines the specific forms required for the registration package.

Sample Registration Information

- Registration date(s)
- Location (City and State)
- Hotel rates, address, number of reserved rooms
- Cut-off date for reduced room rates
- Registration fees by age group
- T-shirt prices by size
- Agenda for each day of the reunion
- Cut-off date for registration

You are on your way to success. You have completed the chapter on registration. Although it is a brief chapter, it is an important part of planning a reunion. Use the resources available to you. The sample registration package, located in the Index of Forms, will assist your team in preparing for your reunion.

Chapter 5 Summary: Key Areas Addressed

- Registration for a family reunion should be an organized process, and it starts with confirmation of key information.
- I recommend you use a tracking system for

reunion registration. The system can be a simple binder or a computerized system.
- Registration information must be accurate. Misinformation causes multiple problems such as family confusion, increased reunion expenses, tension amongst team members, delays in targeted dates for tasks completion and much, much more.
- A sample registration package, consisting of four documents, listed below, is available in the Index of Forms. We use these sample documents for our family reunions.

1. Registration Letter
2. Registration Form
3. T-shirt Form
4. Request for Auction Gift Form

CHAPTER 6

REUNION EVENTS

Chapter Preview

- Introduction to the Chapter
- Recommended Activities
- Meet and Greet
- Picnic
- Free Time
- Room Set-up for Banquet
- Banquet
- Chapter Summary: Key Areas Addressed
- Sample Auction Gifts, Descriptions and Starting Bid Documents (See Index of Forms)
- Sample Bidding Log (See Index of Forms)

When planning your reunion events, the planning team should consider activities that are exciting and engaging. The schedule for the events should be flexible, so that participants can flow in and out of the activities due to arrival times or hotel check-ins. The events discussed in this chapter are customary for my family at our reunions; however, I recommend that engaging family members and friends be your primary focus at your reunion. Be sure to select activities that positively impact the goals for your reunion.

If this is the first time your family is having a reunion, you might scale the events down because of limited participation, financial resources, or other reasons. The planning team has the responsibility of selecting events targeting the overall family. The events listed below provide options for your planning team.

Meet and Greet

The Meet and Greet can set the tone for the reunion. There is generally much excitement in reconnecting with family members from previous reunions and in seeing the faces of first-time attendees. The Meet and Greet is the initial celebration. Family members and friends can introduce themselves with expressions of love through hugs, kisses, and maybe even tears.

The activities for the events are flexible. We encourage

individuals to take part in different activities throughout the event. The sample activities, listed below, are customary for my family reunion's Meet and Greet.

Sample Activities

- Registration
- T-shirt pick up
- Self-Introduction
- Table Games
- Group Discussion
- Overview of Reunion
- Self-Serve Light Snacks

Picnic

A reunion picnic is often full of fun activities and great food. You should seriously assess the decision to have a picnic. You want to assess factors such as the weather, facility, reunion location, and other factors. For example, planning a picnic in New Orleans, Louisiana, may not be ideal. New Orleans is known for its tourism. The city has 15 top locations for tours, a variety of sightseeing areas, and a host of markets. A picnic can be exciting, but it can be money not wisely spent, if family members elect to go on tours or sightseeing ventures, to the market, or to other places instead of attending the picnic.

A picnic provides opportunities to engage in outdoor

physical activities, especially if a large percent of reunion participants are young adults and children. Always be mindful of the fact that activities should also accommodate the elderly and physically challenged. If you decide to plan a picnic, please consider using a facility in compliance with the ADA (Americans with Disability Act).

If you plan a picnic and a banquet for the reunion, I recommend not holding these activities on the same day. Having both events on the same day creates a high probability for conflict with the banquet set-up schedule. The overlapping of assignments for a picnic and a banquet on the same day can cause concerns regarding exhaustion of the planning team.

If the team is planning a picnic, I recommend the picnic be combined with the meet and greet. The activities for both events are similar, with exception of a cook-out at the picnic. These events are sometimes combined for our family reunion.

Free Time

Free time is simple free time. It is a block of time where family and friends have the option to choose their own activities such as going on tours, sightseeing, shopping, catching a nap, meeting family and friends for a small gathering, or just going out for a walk.

Free time gives individuals the flexibility to select activities of his or her choosing. It is what you do with it. However, you should remind those who have volunteered for tasks of the specific times and locations to meet for their instructions.

Room Set-up for Banquet

The room preparation for banquet activities can be a delightful part of the reunion. The room set-up team may include the venue's set-up staff, the reunion planning team, board representatives, and other volunteers. Just setting up for the banquet is a wonderful method of engaging family and friends. This engagement could set the tone for future reunions to occur at the venue.

The approved floor plan should be the guide for setting up the space for activities. It should also serve as the monitoring tool for the planning team. For example, the approved plan may state the venue should set up an elevated head-table, but the work crew decided to set up a standard head-table. The approved floor plan is part of the contract, and the planning team may request a change in the set-up of the head-table.

Banquet

The banquet is customarily the main event of a family reunion. The program for a banquet will vary from family to family. Prior to contract negotiation, I recommend that you create a draft program to identify any needed equipment, space, special set-up, and other items. You should discuss the required item in the first meeting with venue representative. The items negotiated for the banquet should be listed in the contract. I recommend several program activities below, which are traditional for our family reunion.

Welcome:

Let everyone know they are appreciated for taking park in the reunion and you are looking forward to their ongoing participation.

Acknowledgment of Head Table:

Elderly family members and friends are usually selected for the head table. Some families celebrate the head table individuals with gifts, introductions, name placement cards, and even serve their meals. The planners may also have an elevated head table with special decoration.

Memorial Candlelight:

This is a special activity celebrating deceased loved ones. It can truly be memorable, even though there are often tears. The planning team may involve the youth carrying candles as information is shared commemorating family members.

Buffet Dinner:

The buffet dinner is a special meal prepared for the reunion. Family members have the flexibility to interact with each other as they serve themselves.

Auction:

The auction must be well-planned. Family members and friends mostly donate the auction gifts. Oftentimes, family members request donated gifts from organizations. This can be an activity with great financial return. Money raised from the auction can be used for the next reunion's start-up costs, college scholarships, and other worthwhile causes. The sample documents (Bidding Log, and Auction Gift with Description and Starting Bid), located in the Index of Forms, can assist you in getting started with this activity. These documents are used for our family reunions.

Recognition:

This activity has a personal impact on participants and is generally conducted by the Team Leader for the Reunion. Areas of focus may include those listed below.

- First-time attendees
- Individual traveling the longest distance: This individual may receive a small gift

- Introduction of Local Planning Team: Members may be introduced by name or as a group
- Other comments as determined

Closing Remarks: General Chairperson

Areas of focus may include:

- Selecting the Planning Team for the next reunion
- Confirmation of next reunion's location and date(s)
- Special announcements
- Introduction of Board of Directors (by name, position, city, and state)
- Introduction of evaluation process for reunion

Evaluation of Reunion:

- Evaluation Forms are distributed by the team to all participants.
- A designated location and time should be provided for collecting completed form.
- All completed forms should be submitted to the team leader.

Dancing:

Everyone will have the opportunity to showcase their moves! There is routinely a DJ playing music throughout the banquet.

Family members and friends show their enjoyment of the reunion by participating in the activities of various events.

Chapter 6 Summary: Key Areas Addressed

- The planning team should consider events that have engaging and exciting activities for a family reunion.
- The overlapping of assignments for a picnic and banquet on the same day can cause concerns regarding exhaustion of the planning team.
- A reunion planning team has the responsibility to select events targeting the overall family. The events listed below are customary for our family reunions.

1. Meet and Greet
2. Picnic
3. Free Time
4. Room Set-up for Banquet
5. Banquet

   - A banquet is usually considered the highlight of

the reunion that includes a variety of activities.
- The sample forms for this chapter, located in the Index of Forms, are examples used for our family reunions.

CHAPTER 7
REUNION BUDGET

Chapter Preview

- Introduction to the Chapter
- Projecting Income and Expenses
- Using a Line-Item Budget as Monitoring Tool
- Options for Start-up Funds
- Chapter Summary: Key Areas Addressed
- Sample Projected Budget (See Index of Forms)
- Sample Details for Projected Income (See Index of Forms)
- Sample Vendor Receipt Form (See Index of Forms)

A budget is a critical tool for planning a reunion. I recommend using a detailed, line-item budget, and it should clearly outline the projected income and expenditures. To start the budget, consider answering the questions below. The list of questions for each area is not exhaustive but will start the thought process for determining both income and expenses.

Projecting Reunion Income

- Have you established the age groups for reunion fees?
- What is the projected income for each age group?
- What is the combined projected income for all reunion fees?
- What is the projected income for the 50/50 raffle?
- What is the projected income for raffle tickets?
- What is the projected income for t-shirts?
- Will your start-up funds be a donation or a loan?
- What is the projected amount needed for start-up funds?
- What is the amount of carryover funds from the previous reunion?
- What is the projected income for the auction?
- What is the total projected income?

Projecting Reunion Expenses

- What is the projected expense for the venue(s)?
- What is the deposit amount for the venue(s)?
- What is the projected expense for the DJ?
- What is the projected expense for the t-shirts?
- What is the deposit for the t-shirts?
- What is the projected expense for food (banquet)?
- What is the projected expense for Meet and Greet and the Picnic?
- What is the projected expense for the photographer?
- What is the projected expense for printing?
- What is projected expense for miscellaneous items?

A line-item budget is an excellent monitoring tool for income and expenses, and you must exercise discipline as you plan the reunion. Until you receive the income, it is only a projection, and therefore, the expenses must be monitored. If there are indicators that the projected income will be less, you must decrease the projected expenses.

Start-up cost and start-up funds are often overlooked when establishing plan for a family reunion. However, the three options recommend below can be a solution for securing start-up funds.

Option 1: Start-up funds for a family reunion can be secured by obtaining donations from family members. You should reflect the donations in the budget as income.

Option 2: Start-up funds can be secured by obtaining a loan, most often from family members, and must be reflected in the budget as income and as an expense.

Option 3: Start-up funds can be secured from using carryover funds from previous reunions and should be reflected in the budget as income.

A sample projected budget, sample details for projected income, and sample receipt for payment of vendors are located in the Index of Forms. The information serves as a guide for reunion planners, and the documents are examples used during our family reunions. Now that you understand the budget process, you want the entire team to be in agreement, and understand the importance of operating within the budget.

Chapter 7 Summary: Key Areas Addressed

- A budget is a critical tool in planning a reunion, and it should clearly detail the projected income and expenses.
- To start your reunion budget consider responding

Engaging the Family: Reunion Planning Made Simple

to the list of questions for projected income and expenses located in this chapter.
- This chapter provides three recommended options to secure start-up funds for a reunion.
- The funds generated from fundraising activities can help defray reunion expenses, including start-up costs.
- A line-item budget is an excellent tool for monitoring income and expenses.

CHAPTER 8
REUNION MONITORING

Chapter Preview

- Introduction to the Chapter
- Effective Monitoring
- Overview of Reunion Task Checklist
- Chapter Summary: Key Areas Addressed
- Sample Reunion Task Checklist (See Index of Forms)
- Sample Communication Request (See Index of Forms)

Monitoring is a process used to track the progress toward targeted tasks. It is an essential component of planning a family reunion, and one strategy that should be used throughout the planning process. Monitoring keeps the planning team on-target in all areas, including tasks that must be achieved in the initial planning stages. Those tasks include selecting the reunion dates, location (city, state), and venue.

Staying on target is a primary goal. Therefore, monitoring throughout the development and execution of reunion plans will keep the planning team on target. Effective monitoring is a process that provides the planning team with the status of plans at any given time. The more organized the team, the smoother the process will be in executing targeted plans.

When planning a reunion, it is vital to the success of the reunion to establish tasks timelines, and to work within those timelines. You need a monitoring tool that keeps the team focused on tasks and timelines. You may want to develop a master calendar, listing the tasks and timelines for your reunion.

A sample Reunion Task Checklist, which I highly recommend for monitoring a family reunion, is located in the Index of Forms. The Checklist is a simple tool designed specifically for monitoring the planning of a reunion. It is user-friendly, and allows team members to establish timelines, self-monitor, monitor each other, list follow-up tasks, and add new tasks. It can feel odd to have others monitoring you, but that is just part of being on a team like this one.

In reviewing the Reunion Tasks Checklist, you will request that the venue contact person address several tasks. Therefore, I recommend a written communication request, addressing all applicable areas, be sent to the venue representative. A sample Communication Request is located in the Index of Forms.

Chapter 8 Summary: Key Areas Addressed

- Monitoring is a process used to track the progress of targeted tasks, and is also an essential component of planning a family reunion.
- When planning a reunion, it is vital to the success of the reunion to establish task timelines, and work within the timelines.
- The planning team needs a monitoring tool that keeps the team focused on tasks and timelines.
- A Sample Reunion Checklist is located in the Index of Forms. It is an example used during our family reunions.
- A Sample Communication Request Form is located in the Index of Forms. This document is also used for our family reunions.

CHAPTER 9
BOARD OF DIRECTORS

Chapter Preview

- Introduction to the Chapter
- Vision and Goals
- Roles and Responsibilities
- Chapter Summary: Key Areas Addressed
- Sample Membership
- 1990-2020 Reunion Locations

You should select board members very carefully, taking into account the vision and goals you have established for your reunion. The primary function of the board is to ensure the achievement of the family's vision and goals. We adopted the sample vision and goals stated below for our family reunions.

Vision

To host family reunions that will connect and reconnect family members throughout the world.

Goals

1. To implement strategies that intentionally engage our biological and extended family members.
2. To use proven procedures and tools in planning reunions.
3. To plan and host affordable reunions and provide start-up funds for the next reunion.

Based on my experience, having a board of directors is not a common practice for family reunions. However, the structure of our family reunion is designed for board members to works closely with the planning team, in order to fulfill the intended purpose of connecting and reconnecting family members. We align the responsibilities of board members to the vision and goals for reunions.

If your family has a board of directors, I strongly recommend membership be comprised of family members from various cities and states. This recommendation is based on the configuration of membership for our board of directors. Having a board with representation from various cities and states contributes to increased reunion participation.

We view family members showing a commitment to the

reunion's established vision and goals as excellent candidates for board members. The commitment is assessed through their history of volunteering for fundraising activities, attending reunions, assisting with events at reunions, assisting elderly family members and friends at banquets, and other instances where they have shown family reunions are important to them.

Members of the board of directors can make an impact on family members who take part in the reunions. In 1996, we established the board of directors with 7 members. The membership represented 6 states. In 2016, the board membership increased to 11. The board members have directly assisted in the increase of participation in family reunions. Based on records for the 1990 reunion, there were 94 participants, representing 11 cities and 6 states. The 2018 reunion records show 276 participants, which is an increase of 182 reunion participants. The 276 participants represented 51 cities and 19 states.

Further in this chapter, you will see the document representing the board membership for the Turner/Ford Family reunions. The document provides the names, roles, cities, and states of board members. These individuals are dedicated and committed to the vision and goals for our family's reunions. They demonstrate their dedication and commitment through the execution of their assigned roles and responsibilities, which you will also find further in this chapter.

Although the board plays a vital role in the reunion, it is

the planning team that provides the glue that holds it all together. Achieving the reunion's vision and goals should be the focus throughout the planning process.

The leadership of the planning team and leadership of the board of directors have exciting and engaging roles. They are responsible for keeping their team focused on the vision and goals established for the family reunions. Because of their responsibilities, I strongly recommend a co-leader for each position.

A co-leader is essential in planning major projects. I learned the lesson the hard way. The lesson I learned came after being admitted to the hospital with no trained back-up person for a major project. The purpose of a back-up person or co-leader is to share information when there is no team meeting, assume leadership role in the event team leader has an emergency, and make decisions when holding a team meeting is not practical.

Overall, the leadership and co-leadership in planning and executing plans with team members for a family reunion should show levels of dedication, commitment, and a love for family and friends. The labor of love contributes to the reunion being memorable, enjoyable, successful, and celebratory.

Roles and Responsibilities

There are clearly defined roles and responsibilities for members of the board. Fulfilling their responsibilities contributes to overall growth in all areas of the family reunions. As you review the roles and responsibilities of the board members, I hope you will understand the effect of these roles on the vision and goals of the family reunion.

General Chairperson:

- Communicates with the board members in all areas of reunion planning and execution.
- Conducts board meetings and helps maintain reunion records.
- Works with all board members to maintain focus on the family's vision and goals for reunions.
- Engages with board members by utilizing their skills to ensure successful reunions.
- Helps identify family members not attending reunions and provides information to the family tracing team.
- Supports the planning team and board members in setting up the auction.
- Assists board members in their specific roles as needed.
- Other tasks as required.

Co-General Chairperson:

- Provides support to the general chairperson in conducting meetings, including preparation of

meeting materials, recording minutes of board meetings, etc.
- Communicates with and assists local planning team regarding the meet and greet.
- Oversees the set-up for auction gifts and activities,
- Assists with fundraising activities, and supports assistant treasurer in collecting bids for auction gifts and other fundraising activities.
- Maintains focus on the family's vision and goals for reunions.
- Secures gifts for fundraising activities.
- Other tasks as required.

Memorial Chairperson and Co-Chairperson:

- Oversees, with support of co-chairperson, the activities commemorating deceased family members.
- Maintains focus on the family's vision and goals for reunions.
- Identifies family members not attending reunions and gives information to the family tracing team.
- Helps secure gifts for auction and other fundraising activities.
- Secures names of deceased family members for memorial commemoration.
- Helps with setting up for auction and raffle.

- Identifies participants assisting in memorial candlelight activity.
- Other tasks as required.

Fundraising Chairperson and Co-Chairperson:

- Oversees the raffle and fundraising activities at the meet and greet and banquet.
- Maintains focus on the family's vision and goals for reunions.
- Helps secure supplies (i.e. raffle tickets, auction paddles, etc.) for fundraising activities.
- Conducts raffle drawings with support of the fundraising team.
- Communicates fundraising procedures to the team regarding distribution of raffle tickets and reporting of funds to assistant treasurer.
- Engages family members and friends to maximize the sale of raffle tickets.
- Identifies family members not attending reunion and provides information to the family tracing team.
- Other tasks as required.

Head-Table Chairperson:

- Communicates with the treasurer to obtain

names and other information for head-table guests.
- Completes set-up for the head table with gifts, name placements, etc. with support from board members.
- Notifies head table participants of their seating arrangement.
- Recruits volunteers at reunion to assist with head table tasks (seating, etc.).
- Makes introduction of head table participants to family members and friends.
- Maintains focus on the family's vision and goals for reunion.
- Identifies family members not attending reunion and provides information to the family tracing team.
- Other tasks as required.

Family Tracer Chairperson and Co-Chairperson:

- Oversees family tracing with support of the co-chairperson and board members.
- Works with the treasurer in developing a mailing list of newly connected family members and friends.
- Communicates with newly connected family members and friends.

- Maintains focus on the family's vision and goals for reunions.
- Assists in securing donated gifts for auction, head table, and raffles.
- Helps with table set up for auction gifts, including writing description of gifts.
- Provides information to treasurer regarding potential head table quests.
- Other tasks as required.

Treasurer:

- Oversees reunion finances with support from assistant treasurer and general chairperson.
- Maintains all financial records for the family reunion, including reunion bank account.
- Disburses funds for reunion activities with support from general chairperson.
- Helps secure and organize gifts for auction, and other fundraising activities.
- Supports the family tracing team in maintaining data for family and friends.
- Helps with table set up for auction gifts, including writing description of gifts.
- Maintains focus on the family's vision and goals for family reunions.
- Other tasks as required.

Assistant Treasurer:

- Assists the treasurer in financial matters as needed.
- Oversees the finances for the auction and other fundraising activities during the family reunion.
- Supports planning team in securing gifts for auction, and maintains bidding log for auction gifts.
- Reconciles auction bids with funds received and submits a report to the treasurer.
- Communicates with the general chairperson and treasurer regarding reunion finances.
- Maintains focus on the family's vision and goals for family reunions.
- Supports tracing team in identifying family members not attending reunions.
- Other tasks as required.

Historian:

- Responsibilities shared between General Chairperson, Treasurer, and other board members.
- Maintains documents from each reunion, such as sign-in sheets, copies of programs, itineraries, reunion pictures, registration documents, etc.
- Communicates with other board members as

necessary in securing family information and documents from reunions.

This chapter summarizes the board of director's function, their contributions to the reunion through their roles and responsibilities, and the impact they have on achieving the vision and goals of family reunions.

1990-2020 Turner/Ford Family Reunion Locations

1990	Marvin Joiner and Steve Joiner Chairpersons	Memphis	Tennessee
1992	Donald and Bettie Milledge Chairpersons	Romulus	Michigan
1994	Alice Faye White and James White Chairpersons	Grenada	Mississippi
1996	Clara Bell and Sidney Joseph Chairpersons	Homewood	Illinois
1998	Terroll and Angelia Farries Chairpersons	Atlanta	Georgia
2000	Robert and Pearlie Joseph Chairpersons	Davenport	Iowa
2002	Marvin and Asariner Joiner Chairpersons	Memphis	Tennessee
2004	Terroll and Angelia Farries Chairpersons	Atlanta	Georgia
2006	Ruby White-Walls & Ophelia Bufford Chairpersons	Oxford	Mississippi
2008	Clara Bell and Sidney Joseph Chairpersons	Ford City	Illinois
2010	Terroll and Angelia Farries Chairperson	Atlanta	Georgia
2012	Marvin Joiner and Jacqueline Moore Chairpersons	Memphis	Tennessee
2014	Hazel Davis and Pamela Turner Chairpersons	St. Louis	Missouri
2016	Loraine Williams-Turner & Keyra Harrison Chairpersons	New Orleans	Louisiana
2018	Clara Bell and Sidney Joseph Chairpersons	Tinley Park	Illinois
2020	Cleveland and Rosie Joseph Chairpersons	Oxford	Mississippi

- Reunion cancelled because of COVID-19 pandemic.

Engaging the Family: Reunion Planning Made Simple

Sample Board of Directors Membership: Turner/Ford Family

No.	Name	Role	City	State
1.	Bettie Milledge	General Chairperson	Hiram	Georgia
2.	Angelia Farries	Co-General Chairperson	Hiram	Georgia
3.	Marvin Joiner	Memorial Chairperson	Memphis	Tennessee
4.	Neoykee Wadley	Co-Memorial Chairperson	Oxford	Mississippi
5.	Freddie Harris	Fundraising Chairperson	Seattle	Washington
6.	Sidney Joseph	Co-Fundraising Chairperson	Chicago	Illinois
7.	Hazel Davis	Head-Table Chairperson	St. Louis	Missouri
8.	Clara Bell	Family Tracer Chairperson	Chicago	Illinois
9.	Anita Washington	Co. Family Tracer Chairperson	Chicago	Illinois
10.	Ruby White-Walls	Treasurer	Water Valley	Mississippi
11.	Cleveland Joseph	Assistant Treasurer	Oxford	Mississippi
12.	Aleen Turner (Deceased)	Served: Memorial Chairperson	Las Vegas	Nevada
13.	Alice Faye White (Deceased)	Served: Treasurer	Water Valley	Mississippi

Although team members are not listed, it is important to note the reunions would not have been successful without the TEAM! To all team members, thank you for your support and dedication in planning and hosting each reunion. Always know you are loved and appreciated!

Chapter 9 Summary: Key Areas Addressed

- You should select a board member carefully, taking into account the vision and goals established for your reunion.
- The board of directors works closely with the planning team to fulfill the intended purpose of connecting and reconnecting family members.
- You can assess a potential board member through their history of volunteering for fundraising, assisting with events at reunions, assisting elderly family members and friends at banquets, etc.
- The board plays a vital role in the reunion, but it is the planning team providing the glue that seals the reunion.
- As board members fulfill their roles and responsibilities, they contribute to the overall growth of family reunions.
- The sample documents (Located in the Index), Turner/Ford Board of Directors Membership, and 1990-2020 Family Reunion Locations, are examples for our family reunions.

CHAPTER 10
ASSESSING THE REUNION

Chapter Preview

- Introduction of the Chapter
- Purpose of Evaluation
- Chapter Summary: Key Areas Addressed
- Sample Reunion Evaluation Form (See Index of Forms)

Assessing the reunion is the last step in the process. An evaluation form is one way of documenting the outcome of each reunion. It gives you a quick glance of how well the reunion plan was executed.

On the last day of the reunion, distribute an evaluation form to each participant for completion. Then collect them to create a tally summary sheet. The summary tally can reveal areas of your reunion that could benefit from a change. The summary tally and individual tally sheets should be maintained by the team leader, treasurer, or other designated individuals.

For family historical purposes, you need to know the outcome of each reunion: who attended (sign-in sheets and pictures), what the activities were (agenda), how participants felt about the reunion, what the program was like, what foods were served, etc. Years from now, as you reflect on your family reunions, you will have authentic documents to support your memories.

Chapter 10 Summary: Key Areas Addressed

- An evaluation of the reunion gives you a quick glance of how well the plan was executed.
- For historical purposes, you need to know the outcome of each reunion.
- The Sample Evaluation Form is located in the Index of Forms.

INDEX OF FORMS

The sample forms identified in each Chapter, listed below, are located in this Section.

- Chapter 2: Family Reunion Survey
- Chapter 3: Request to Host Family Reunion
- Chapter 4: Venue Survey
- Chapter 5: Reunion Letter, Registration, Reunion T-shirt, Request for Auction Gift
- Chapter 6: Auction Gifts Descriptions & Starting Bids, Auction Bidding Log
- Chapter 7: Projected Budget, Details for Projected Income, Vendor Receipt
- Chapter 8: Reunion Task Checklist, Communication Request
- Chapter 10: Reunion Evaluation

Sample Family Reunion Survey (Chapter 2)

Date: _____ Email: _____

Name: _____ Phone #: _____

City: _____ State: _____ Zip Code: _____

Note: Greet family member with a high level of enthusiasm and share the nature of your call.

Sample Script (Nature of call): I have been thinking about our family having a reunion. I want to follow through on the idea, but I need your input and help.

START ASKING YOUR QUESTIONS.

1. What are your thoughts on our family having a reunion?
   _____

2. Are you willing to take part in a meeting to discuss having a family reunion?
   _____

3. When is a good time to follow up with you regarding a family reunion?
   _____

4. Who are family members you recommend I contact regarding a family reunion?

   Name_____ Phone # _____

   Name_____ Phone # _____

   Name_____ Phone # _____

5. If you were planning a reunion where would you have it?
   _____

6. How often are you willing to meet and help plan our family reunion?
   _____

Summarize the survey information and share it at the meeting.

Sample Request to Host a Family Reunion Form (Chapter 3)

Please complete form and return to a board member prior to the board meeting.

1. Planning team information:

    a. Contact Person _____ Phone #: _____

    b. Email _____

2. Proposed Date(s) for Reunion:

    a. Desirable Date(s) _____

    b. Alternative Date(s) _____

3. Proposed Location for Reunion:

    City _____ State _____

4. Experience of Reunion Planning Team:

    a. Does team leader or members of the team, have experience in planning a family reunion? Yes_____ No _____ If yes, provide a brief overview of experience: _____
    _____

    b. If no, are you and your team willing to work directly with the board representatives to plan and host reunion? Yes_____ No _____

5. If the team is selected by the family and or board, will the contact person and at least two team members be available to meet with board representative(s) following the banquet? Yes_____ No _____

6. Please share why your team would like to host the family reunion?
    _____
    _____

Sample Venue Survey Form (Chapter 4)

Date: _____ Name of Venue: _____ Phone #: _____

Address of Venue: _____

City: _____ State: _____ Zip Code: _____

Survey conducted by: _____

The purpose of the survey is to conduct a preliminary assessment to determine the likelihood of hosting a family reunion at venue location.

1. Friendliness of front desk staff via phone call: _____

2. Communication with sales staff: Yes _____ No _____

   * Explain nature of call: Family is planning a reunion and would like to consider hosting the reunion at your venue.
   * Determine availability of date(s) _____ Yes _____ No _____
   * Alternative date(s) available _____ Yes _____ No _____

3. Sales rep willingness to provide a banquet package to team: Yes ____ No ____

   Targeted date to receive banquet package: _____

4. Sales Rep open to negotiating rates (rooms, meals, etc.): Yes _____ No _____

   Record comments regarding negotiation of rates _____
   _____

5. Is there a deposit for venue? Yes _____ $ _____ No _____

6. Sales staff available for tour of facility: Yes _____ Date _____ No _____

7. Other information:
   _____
   _____

Sample Reunion Letter (Chapter 5)

Name of Family Reunion

Date: _____

Dear _____,

    We are delighted to inform you of plans to host a _____. It is our first reunion, and we are extremely excited. As we continue the planning, know that your help is needed to make the reunion successful. The information below will assist you with getting ready to participate in the reunion.

Reunion Date(s): _____

City: _____ State: _____

Hotel: * Name _____

        * Address _____

        * City: _____ State: _____ Zip Code: _____

        * Phone #: _____

When making your room reservation(s), you must request reservation for the

(insert name of family reunion). The hotel room rate (double or king) is $_____

+ tax per night. The hotel has free (list what is free such as parking, etc.). Please reserve your room(s) early. The room cut-off date for reduced rate is _____.

Reunion fees: The team was able to keep the fee structure as low as possible for each age group. **Insert fee for each group if you decide to use the fee structure.**

17 and older	$_____	8-10 years	$_____
14-16 years	$_____	4-7 years	$_____
11-13 Years	$_____	3 years & under	$_____

Page 2: Sample Reunion Letter (Chapter 5)

The reunion fees must be paid in full by (**list date**). Please complete the enclosed Registration Form and return with fee(s) to address provided on the form.

Reunion T-shirt: The T-shirt is a keepsake. Years later, it will remind you of the fun time you had at the reunion. Please complete the enclosed T-shirt Form and return it with your Registration From. Your check or money order can be combined (registration fee(s) and T-shirt fee(s)).

The team has planned a fun packed reunion for family members and friends. Please join us for this celebration. Some of the reunion activities are listed below.

* Welcome – Meet and Greet and or Picnic
* Family Games (indoor and or outdoor games)
* Variety of food, soft drinks, water, etc.
* T-shirt distribution
* Banquet (a celebration dinner)
* Raffle and or Auction
* Other activities

If you have any questions, please do not hesitate to give me a call at phone number _____ or email me at _____.
We are ready to celebrate our family and friends. We look forward to a glorious reunion with heartfelt fellowship.

On behalf of the Planning Team, be blessed and we hope to see you at the family reunion.

Sincerely,

Name Chairpersons

Sample Reunion Registration Form (Chapter 5)

The (Family Name _____ 20___ _ Family Reunion

We must receive this form no later than (date)_____ with check or money order.

Contact Name: _____ Phone #: _____ Date: _____

Address: _____ Apt. #: _____

City: _____ State: _____ Zip Code: _____

Email: _____

No	Name (List all names covered by payment)	Age Group	Fee
1.			
2.			
3.			
4.			
5.			

Fee(s): 17 Years & Older $ _____   Please send completed forms

      14-16 Years $ _____   (registration and t-shirt) with check or

      11-13 Years $ _____   money order to:

      8-10 Years $ _____   Name: _____

      4-7 Years $ _____   Address: _____

      3 yrs. & Under $ _____   City: _____ State: ____ Zip Code_____

Sample Reunion T-Shirt Order Form (Chapter 5)

We must receive this form no later than (Date)_____ with check or money order.

Contact Person: _____ Phone #: _____

Group	Size	Size	Size	Size	Total T-shirt	Unit Price	*Total Price
Youth	Extra Small (2-4)	Small (6-8)	Medium (10-12)	Large (14-16)		Unit Price X Total T-shirt = TP*	
						$10.00	
Adult	Small	Medium	Large	Extra Large			
						$12.00	
Custom	2X	*******	*******	*******		$13.00	
	3X	*******	*******	*******		$14.00	
	4X	*******	*******	*******		$15.00	
	5X	*******	*******	*******		$16.00	
Grand Total							

T-shirts will be distributed to the contact person listed on the order form.

Signature: _____ Date: _____

Please send your t-shirt order form with your registration form. See address listed on registration form.

Sample Auction Gift Form (Chapter 5)

Please consider donating a gift for the auction. Your support will help reduce the cost of future reunions.

Gift Donated by: _____

Contact Number: _____

Email: _____

Name of Gift: _____

Description of Gift: _____

_____

Starting Bid for Gift: $ _____

Please bring your gift to the reunion and give it to: _____

Thank you for your support!

The Reunion Planning Team

Sample Auction Gifts, Descriptions and Starting Bids (Chapter 6)

1. **YOUNG CHIEF BASKET**: Starting Bid- $35.00

   If you enjoy making special items, this basket is for you or your young chief. The basket contains:

   * Cup Cake Maker   * Dish Towels   * Mixing Spoons
   * Waffle Maker   * Cup Cake & Waffle Mixes * Measuring Cups
   * Corn Dog Make   * Mixing cups   * Toppings for Cup Cakes

2. **Cooking Center Basket: Starting Bid - $50.00**

   This 3in 1 cooking center is ideal for making easy meals. You can fry your bacon, cook your eggs while brewing your coffee, all at the same time. This is a wonderful addition to your kitchen appliances.

3. **Bedding Basket: Starting Bid - $40.00**

   What a deal! This basket contains a 16-piece sheet set for a king size bed. The colors are green and white. This is a great buy. The set has:

   - 4 Flat Sheets
   - 8 Standard Pillowcases
   - 4 Fitted Sheets

4. **Family Heirloom Quilt: Starting Bid – 75.00**

   This heirloom represents 9 family reunions. The T-shirts are reminders of the cities and state where reunions were hosted. The rainbow of colors is breath-taking. The color squares were signed by family members at various reunions.

Sample bidding Log (Chapter 6)

Date: _____

No.	Name of Gift	Final Bid	Payment Received
1.			
2.			
3.			
4.			
5.			
6.			
7.			
8.			
9.			
10.			
11.			
12.			
13.			
14.			
15.			
16.			
17.			
18.			

(Person completing Bidding Log) : _____

Sample Details for Projected Income (Chapter 7)

This information supports income projection based on 150 participants.

Registration Fees:

Age Group	No	Fee	Total	Donations
17 years & older	102	$ 50.00	5100.00	$325.00
14-16 years	20	$ 40.00	800.00	
11-13 years	15	$ 35.00	525.00	
8-10 years	10	$ 30.00	300.00	
4-7 years	3	$ 25.00	75.00	
3 years and under	----	0	0	

Projected Income (Registration Fees): $6800.00

T-Shirt Orders:

Size	No.	Price	Total
Youth	10	$10.00	$ 100.00
Adults	114	$12.00	$1368.00
2X	15	$13.00	$ 195.00
3X	5	$14.00	$ 70.00
4X	3	$15.00	$ 45.00
5X	3	$16.00	$ 48.00

Projected Income for T-shirts $1826.00

Auction Gifts			50/50 Raffle	Meet & Greet Raffle
No of Gifts	Starting Bid	Total	Goal	Goal
30 X	$35.00	$1050.00	$250.00	$100.00

Sample Vendor Receipt Form (Chapter 7)

Acknowledgement of Payment

I, _____, acknowledge receipt of payment for

      (Print Vendor's full name)

_____ provided for the

                     (List services)

_____, based on the written agreement of

      (Family Reunion Name)

$_____.

  (List Dollar Amount)

Signature: _____ Date: _____

                (Vendor)

Signature: (Witness of Payment): _____ Date: _____

Sample Projected Budget   Date: _____ (Chapter 7)

The Budget is based on 150 participants: See details for projected income.

No.	Expense Item	$ Amount	Income Item	$ Amount
1.	Start-up Cost Deposit(s)	900.00	Carryover funds	2100.00
2.	Meet & Greet of Picnic	1500.00	Auction	1050.00
3.	Postage & Envelopes (2 Mailings)	150.00	Donations	325.00
4.	T-shirt Deposit	300.00	Raffle Tickets	100.00
5.	T-shirt (minus deposit)	1526.00	T-shirts	1826.00
6.	Disc Jockey	250.00	50/50 Raffle	250.00
7.	Banquet (Food)	5032.50	Reunion Fees Registration	6800.00
8.	Photographer	300.00		
9.	Bane Tags	25.00		
10.	Printing: Flyers & Program	150.00		
11.	Memorial: Candles and Plaques, etc.	125.00		
12.	50/50 Raffle	125.00		
13.	Miscellaneous	200.00		
14.	Total Expenses	10,583.50		$12,451.00
	Projected Net Income			

$10,583.50 - $12,451.00 = $1867.50 (Projected Net Income)

Sample Reunion Task Checklist (Chapter 8)

Planning team should focus on applicable tasks. They are not in order of execution.

No.	Recommended Task	Target Date	Team Member	Follow-up Tasks	Comment
1.	Team Leader should establish planning team				
2.	Confirm reunion date(s) and location (City and State)				
3.	Determine projected number of attendees & hotel rooms per day				
4.	Draft Banquet Program: Needed to know equip. room set-up, etc.				
5.	Identify proposed venue(s) and request reunion package				
6.	Meet with venue representatives to discuss/negotiate reunion package, rates – hotel rooms, parking, activity space, etc. (free activity space is the goal)				
7.	Select potential venue/hotel for reunion: Discuss banquet not being next door to a live band!!				
8.	Discuss venue/hotel for reunion with team members				
9.	Request timeframe to receive proposed contract and floor plan for banquet				
10.	Review proposed contract to make sure items agreed upon in meeting are included (in contract)				
11.	Team leader discusses proposed contract with general chairperson and treasurer				
12.	Finalize contract with selected venue; need dates, room rates, etc. to prepare registration package				

Sample Reunion Task Checklist (Chapter 8)

13.	Develop Registration Package: Letter, Forms, Request for Gift, etc.				
14.	Send 1st Mailing to Family and friends: Registration Package				
15.	Send 2nd Mailing to family and friends: Reminder with registration information				
16	Develop a proposed menu for banquet (based on negotiated meal allotment in contract)				
17.	Communicate with Venue contact to determine requirements for DJ (Union Membership, Liability Ins, etc.)				
18.	Secure vendor for T-shirts (written agreement and deposit amount)				
19.	Secure photographer and written agreement with deposit amount) Stay within budget				
20.	Develop Flyer for Meet and Greet, and Picnic with planned activities				
21.	Select DJ and secure written agreement (stay within budget) Notify DJ of hotel Requirements				
22.	Submit 1st order for T-shirts and secure cut-off date for ordering				

Sample Reunion Task Checklist (Chapter 8)

23.	Assess T-shirt order to determine need for additional (t-shirts) and submit final order.				
24.	Assign team members specific responsibilities for reunion activities (Meet & Greet, Picnic, Banquet, etc.)				
25.	Communicate with board members to ensure coordination of roles based on reunion activities				
26.	Confirm number of gifts for auction with Treasure: At least 30 with an average bid of $35; make sure written description and starting bids are on each gift				
27.	Communicate with co-general chairperson to confirm Auctioneer and time required to conduct auction (based on number of gifts)				
28.	Request venue / hotel to secure information for tours and other attractions				
29.	Complete program for Banquet and notify individuals of their assignment and approximate time allotted for activity				
30.	Establish time with hotel rep for Set-up of banquet room, including banquet activities - Auction tables, Raffle table, memorial table, etc.				

Sample Reunion Tasks Checklist (Chapter 8)

31.	Communicate with Treasurer regarding gifts for head-table guests				
32.	Notify Treasurer of required checks for Vendors (DJ, photographer, etc.)				
33.	Secure date from venue representative for final meal count (banquet)				
34.	Communicate with hotel representative to ensure sufficient rooms for individuals attending the reunion				
35.	Communicate frequently with Treasurer or individual addressing registration to monitor number of attendees at reunion (count all guest – including 3 and under for seating)				
36.	Communicate with chairperson for memorial activities to ensure readiness for presentation				
37.	**C**ommunicate with venue contact person to ensure microphone, podium, center pieces, color scheme, etc., for banquet				
38.	If underground parking, request height of parking structure and include in registration information				

Sample Reunion Task Checklist (Chapter 8)

39.	Develop schedule for regular team meetings, with agenda items addressing reunion				
40.	Add your new items as needed!				
41.					
42.					
43.					
44.					
45.					
46.					

Sample Communication Request (Chapter 8)

Date _____

Dear (List Venue Representative) _____,

This letter is seeking responses to questions, which are listed below, on behalf of the Planning Team for the (name of family reunion) _____.

The responses will assist the team in monitoring completion of tasks and execution of the reunion plan.

QUESTIONS:

1. Are there any requirements such as union membership, liability insurance, etc. for the DJ?
2. Will the hotel secure information for tours, sightseeing, shopping areas, etc. for family reunion participants?
3. Will the Reunion Planning Team and volunteers be able to set-up banquet activities while the venue team is setting up for reunion banquet?
4. If the parking is underground, what is the height of the structure for each level?
5. What is the final date for the banquet food count?

We thank you for your ongoing support in the helping us to have a successful reunion. As always, we appreciate your timely response.

Sincerely,

Names _____   _____

Chairpersons

Sample Evaluation Form (Chapter 10)

_____   _____
                Reunion Name   Date(s)

1. How did you feel about the overall environment of the reunion?

    _____ Warm and Inviting   _____ Somewhat Cold

2. How about the length of the reunion?   _____ Too Long   _____ Too Short

    _____ Perfect

3. Were the number of reunion activities sufficient? _____ Too Many ____ Too Few

    _____ Perfect

4. What was your favorite activity? _____

5. What was your least favorite activity? _____

6. What would you like to see more of? _____

7. What were your children's favorite activities? _____
_____

8. What was your favorite food? _____

9. What is one thing we should definitely do again at next reunion? _____

10. If you could change one thing about the reunion, what would it be? _____
_____

11. Any suggestions for cutting expenses? _____

12. Do you have other suggestions? _____
_____
_____

ACKNOWLEDGMENTS

To God be the glory! He is worthy to be praised. Father, thank you for the vision, inspiration, and dedication to write this book.

To my wonderful husband, Donald, I thank you for your prayers, patience, dinners, understanding, and loving support. Although there were many nights I retired to bed late after completing typing tasks, compiling information, organizing my thoughts and ideas, you never complained. Your encouragement truly inspired me to complete this book. You are the wind beneath my wings.

I thank my daughter, Angelia Farries, and my teenage granddaughter, Alina Farries, for their support in reading the manuscript and for their encouragement throughout the process of writing this book. A special thank you to Alina for her technology skills and being available when I needed help.

To Betty Smith, my colleague, my friend, and my sister in Christ, thank you for your support. You have been there for me during my professional career and my business, during family challenges, and throughout writing this book. Your encouraging comments, recommendations, and editing of this book are priceless.

Love and blessings to my dear friends. Thank you for your listening ears as I talked about this book, and its intent. May God continue to shower you with His love and blessings.

To the Turner-Ford Family, my family, thank you for "Setting the Tone" for writing this book. You demonstrated the "Fruit of the Spirit" (Love, Joy, Peace, Patience, Kindness, Goodness, Faithfulness, and Self-Control – Galatians 5: 22-23) in connecting and reconnecting family and friends. With much love, THANK YOU!

ABOUT THE AUTHOR

BETTIE MILLEDGE, BORN AND RAISED IN WATER VALLEY, Mississippi, was raised to value family unity, even through adversity. As she grew in years, her family's love, support, and hope kept her grounded.

Bettie took with her the memories of her Water Valley upbringing as she left home. She remembered hearing about the inner strengths of her ancestors, laughing and crying with family during happy times and sad, and the pride she felt through successes. These were the times she remembered and missed being away from home.

Her conversations with family members and friends created a face-to-face environment full of lasting memories. As a result, Bettie became the "brain-child" of the biannual Turner-Ford Family Reunion. These reunions achieve her family's vision to host reunions that connect and reconnect family members and friends throughout the world.

Bettie is a retired educator, organizer, and planner living in Hiram, Georgia with her husband Donald. She is a strong, family-oriented, and giving person known for her love of humankind. She has served as a mentor for young aspiring educators and is credited with mentoring families wanting to plan a family reunion. This book, *Engaging The Family: Reunion Planning Made Simple*, was written as a blueprint for starting and executing a successful reunion.

CAN YOU HELP?

If you found the information in my book helpful, I would greatly appreciate an honest review. I will use your input on future projects.

Please leave your review on Amazon letting me know what you thought of the book.

Thanks so much!

Made in the USA
Columbia, SC
19 March 2021